根気

To my little girl, Nawwara, for introducing me
to the complicated art of tying ponytails,
especially the ones that know jiu-jitsu   —MKA

Thank you, Amir, for your support.
Without it, I could not pursue this dream.   —TH

Special thanks to: My wife, Leena, and son, Zayan | my extended family | my jiu-jitsu families at Maxercise/Ribeiro Philly (USA) and Budo-Schule Waedenswil (Switzerland) | Meredith Elementary School and Nebinger Elementary School communities of Philadelphia | Harry and Julie Kraemer | Anthony and Margo Viscusi | Bill and Gayle Chorske | Omar S. Khawaja, author of the Ilyas & Duck series | All our incredible backers on Kickstarter   —MKA

First Edition, February 2019
10 9 8 7 6 5 4 3 2 1
ISBN 978-1-7328913-0-2

Copyright © 2019 Mir Khalid Ali
Illustrated by Taahira Halim
Cover design by Mir Khalid Ali & Taahira Halim

All rights reserved. Published by Sandfish Press. No part of this book may be reproduced or transmitted in any form or by any means, electronic or mechanical, including photocopying, recording, or by any information storage and retrieval system without written permission from the publisher. For information contact:
Sandfish Press, 238 Queen Street, Unit 1, Philadelphia, PA 19147

Library of Congress Control Number: 2018912373
Ali, Mir Khalid, author
The Jiu-Jitsu Ponytail / by Mir Khalid Ali
Summary: Seven-year-old Noor Karim is preparing to compete in her first jiu-jitsu tournament, but her ponytail refuses to cooperate
ISBN-13: 978-1-7328913-0-2 (hardcover)
ISBN-10: 1-7328913-0-3 (hardcover)

www.JiuJitsuPonytail.com

Printed in China.

February

S	M	T	W	T	F	S
	1 ✗	2 ✗	3 ✗	4 ✗	5 ✗	6 ✗
7 ✗	8 ✗	9 ✗	10 ✗	11 ✗	12 ✗	**13 — Jiu-Jitsu Tournament!!!**
14	15	16	17	18	19	20
21	22	23	24	25	26	27
28						

Just then, several strands of the girl's hair fell on her face.

Without losing focus, she blew at the hair.
"You are ready!" she repeated, staring intently into the mirror.
But her hair tumbled back.

Impatiently, the girl blew again—harder this time—forcing the hair away.

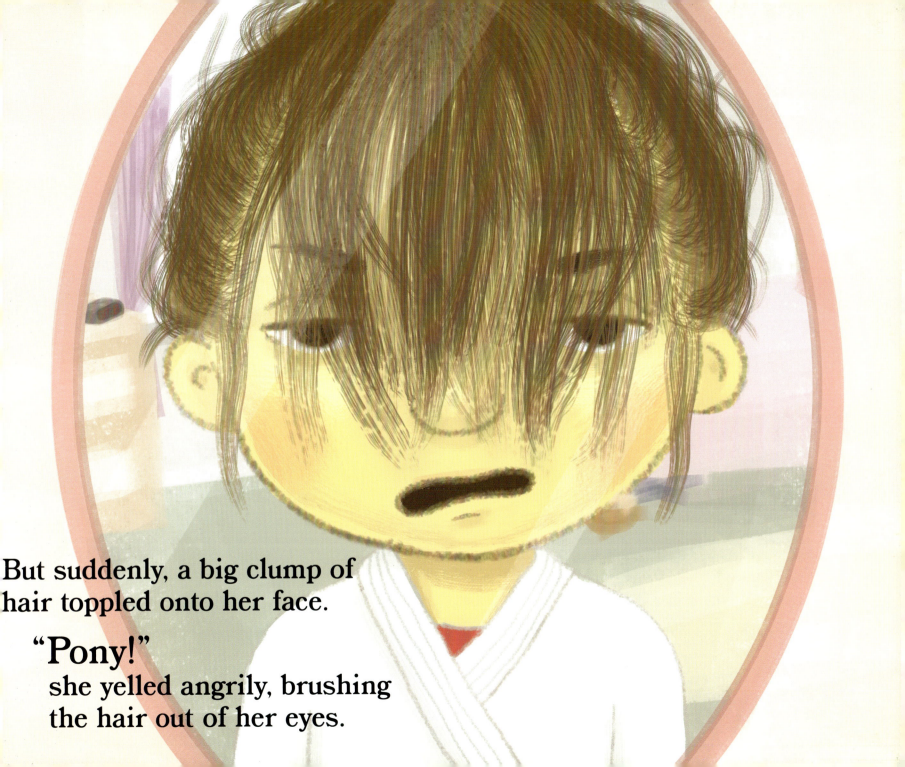

But suddenly, a big clump of hair toppled onto her face.

"Pony!"
she yelled angrily, brushing the hair out of her eyes.

The little girl glared up at her ponytail, which lay slumped sideways in a tangled mess on her head. It yawned and stretched.

It looked like it had just woken up!

"Aargh!" muttered the girl.

She grappled with her ponytail, trying to sweep it together neatly and wrap another hair tie around it.

But her ponytail was having none of that! It flung aside the hair tie and spread out in complete disarray!

But the ponytail fought back! It slipped through the girl's fingers and wrapped around her hand.

Catching the girl by surprise, it hooked one finger and pulled it back.

"Hey!" the girl yelped.

The little girl yanked her trapped finger free. Snatching a handful of bobby pins from her dresser, she tried sticking them into her hair.

But the crafty ponytail twisted and swerved, neatly evading them all!

"Noor!"
The little girl stopped struggling with her ponytail and listened worriedly.

"Hurry up, Noor!" her dad called again from downstairs. "We'll be late for the tournament!"

"Coming, Baba!" the girl yelled back.

Noor had finally had enough! She pulled out a roll of tape and tore off a long strip.

Noor and her father arrived at the jiu-jitsu tournament just in time. They found seats on the bleachers next to Noor's coach and teammates.

"No, I got it!" Noor replied, jumping to her feet.

She bowed and marched onto the mat. Her opponent, a tall, angry-looking girl, stomped onto the mat from the opposite side.

The ponytail took one look at the opponent and started squirming in panic!

Noor and her opponent shook hands. The referee blew the whistle, signaling the start of the match.

"Go, Noor!" her dad and teammates yelled from the bleachers.

Noor's opponent lunged at her, but Noor quickly sidestepped out of the way. Growling in disappointment, her opponent turned and rushed back for another attack!

Noor saw her chance and braced for the right moment to make her move.

Just then, the ponytail broke free from the tape that Noor had wrapped around it, and it caught another sight of the angry girl rushing towards Noor!

The ponytail nearly split all its ends in terror! It grabbed desperately at Noor's face, completely covering her eyes!

Scrambling to shove her hair away, Noor stumbled sideways. Growling happily, Noor's opponent tripped her. She hooked Noor's arm and pulled it back into an arm-bar!

Noor twisted and turned, trying to wrestle free. But it was too late! She had no choice but to tap out. Noor had lost the match.

Noor plodded sadly off the mat. Her dad hugged her.
"You were so brave, Noor!" he said, smiling. "I'm very proud of you!"

But Noor felt terrible. She slumped on the bleachers and covered her face with her hands.

"I just want to go home, Baba," she sobbed.

Noor felt several strands of hair fall on her hands.
"Now what, Pony?" she grumbled.
She ignored her ponytail, but more hair tumbled onto her hands.

"What is it?" Noor finally snapped.

She glared at her ponytail from between her fingers.

And then, Noor remembered.

She remembered how hard she had trained for this tournament, her first one ever.

She remembered how much her friends had helped her and all the hours they had spent practicing together.

And she remembered how her Baba always encouraged her to have faith and never give up.

Slowly, a smile spread across Noor's face.

Noor rummaged in her jiu-jitsu bag and pulled out some hair ties and ribbons.

"Baba," she said, walking over to her dad, "will you please fix up my ponytail?"

"Of course," he replied, smiling.

"I am ready!" declared Noor.

And her ponytail was ready, too!

"Noor Karim!" a tournament official announced.

Noor smiled at her dad, bowed, and stepped onto the mat. This time, her ponytail faced the opponent head-on. It even helped fend off some attacks, and Noor quickly won the match!

Noor's third and fourth matches were much more difficult.

She almost got caught in an arm-bar again!

Another time, she barely escaped from an Americana lock!

But Noor fought hard, and her ponytail whipped out a few jiu-jitsu moves, too!

Together, Noor and her jiu-jitsu ponytail won the last two matches and earned a silver medal for second place!

"You did great today!" Noor's dad grinned as he tucked her into bed that night. "I'm very proud of you, my baby girl!"

"Thanks, Baba!" Noor beamed.

"Oh, do you want me to untie your hair?" her dad asked as he stood up to leave.

"No, thanks, Baba," Noor smiled, "I think I'll keep my jiu-jitsu ponytail for now!"

arm-bar

half-guard

Jiu-Jitsu Practice
with Noor & her Jiu-Jitsu Ponytail

hip throw

side-control

x-guard

omoplata

kimura

closed guard

triangle

hip-escape

double leg takedown

Americana lock

mount

bump and roll escape

about the author

Mir Khalid Ali is an avid traveler, reader, blogger, and foodie. He immigrated to the U.S.A. from Pakistan as a 7-year-old and grew up on a farm in western Pennsylvania. He has been writing stories since he was in 3rd grade. He has a Bachelor of Arts in Political Science from Columbia University in New York and a Masters in Business Administration from the Kellogg School of Management at Northwestern University in Illinois. He is the husband of an outstanding woman and the "Baba" of two amazing kids (along with a number of nieces and nephews who also call him Baba). He lives in Philadelphia with his family, and he and his children have been taking Brazilian jiu-jitsu lessons since 2017. You can learn more about him at www.mirkhalidali.com.

about the illustrator

Taahira Halim is a young artist living in Wilson, North Carolina with her husband. She is trained in early childhood education. An artist by nature, she has produced a variety of artwork over the years. With a growing fascination with and admiration of the power of illustrations to convey stories, she took the full leap into children's book illustration in 2017. "The Jiu-Jitsu Ponytail" is the first full-length book featuring her work. You can learn more about her at www.thalimart.daportfolio.com.